**MARCUS
BUCKINGHAM**

D0547214

THE TRUTH ABOUT YOU

YOUR SECRET TO SUCCESS

THOMAS NELSON
Since 1798

NASHVILLE   DALLAS   MEXICO CITY   RIO DE JANEIRO   BEIJING

CONTENTS

START STRONG

When I was starting out, I didn't know much. I didn't know what I would do with my life. I didn't know what job I really wanted. I didn't even know how I was going to pay my bills.

But I was sure of one thing—I was different from my brother and my sister.

Looking at my older brother and younger sister, I knew I could never be like them. I knew I would never excel at math and science like my brother. I knew I would never match the kind of focus and physical self-discipline my sister relied on to become a ballet dancer. I knew I had my own strengths, and even though I was confused about many things, I was sure that the world was going to wait for me until one day I would pop out of school and make my unique mark on the world.

I bet you feel this way. In school, you knew which subjects you were drawn to, the ones that grabbed your attention and wouldn't let it go, the ones where class time flew by and before you knew it the bell had rung and, though you wouldn't have admitted it to your friends, you almost felt like you wanted to do the class all over again. And even if you didn't like school, you still found yourself drawn to certain situations, certain people, certain times when you knew you were at your best. You might not have called these your "strengths," but from a very early age, you knew you had *something* special to offer.

And now, though you might not know exactly what you want to do with your life, you have faith. You believe in yourself. You yearn for success and achievement, and you're holding out hope that your work will give you the chance to realize these dreams.

Without doubt, work can do this for you. During the last

twenty years, I've interviewed thousands of successful people, and looking through their eyes, work *can* be a great place. A place where you are challenged in just the way you like to be challenged. A place where people recognize you for what you do well and push you to become better and better at it. A place where you get to make the kind of difference only you can make. A place, in the end, where you get to experience the thrill of success.

But I've learned something else too. Fewer than *two out of ten* of us get to play to our strengths at work most of the time. The most successful people do, but only two out of ten get to feel this thrill of success.

I do hundreds of speeches a year, telling people how to spot their strengths and put them to work. They hear the message, they believe it, and they know it's right, but many of them feel as if they've gone too far down the road to do anything about it. They've got their career to think about, bills that keep getting bigger, a growing family, mortgages, promotions. Life has pushed them down a narrowing path, and now they don't feel like they have any freedom to choose.

You'll find this too. You'll find that life gets very heavy, very quickly—and the longer you wait, the heavier it gets. Before you know it, you're pressured into living some second-rate version of your own life. With all the best intentions—to get ahead, to support your family, to pay off your debts—you dive into a job, work hard, get promoted, and then one day you wake up and find yourself in a job that doesn't engage you, that doesn't call on the best of you, a job where you're just marking time, putting in the hours until the weekend comes around again, a job that doesn't give you a kick but instead bores you and burns you out. This job may pay you well. Or, if it doesn't, you may tell yourself that this job will "lead to something better." But, nonetheless, it's a job where, today, at this moment, you feel trapped.

When this happens, as it does to so many of us, you may choose to blame someone else. You may blame your family, your teachers, your organization, or your boss for getting you into this situation. But the responsibility doesn't lie there. It lies with you—and with what you choose to do to take control.

So now, right now, the questions you have to answer are these:

How can I start strong?

How can I become one of the two out of ten people who plays to my strengths and passions most of the time?

How can I create this kind of life for myself, this kind of success?

What do I need to know, and what do I need to do . . . before I get too far down life's path?

In your hands, you're holding the answers to these questions.

First, in the front flap, you'll see there's a film. It's a short film, about twenty minutes. Start by watching it. Without giving too much away, it tells the story of a boy, Ewan, who's faced with a common problem: he's good at something, so the people around him keep telling him to stick to it, but he resists because he feels his strengths pushing him in a different direction. What should he do? Take a stand for his strengths, or do what others expect him to do?

If you haven't been in this situation already, you will be soon. The world is full of "shoulds." Your parents and your teachers look at what you're good at, and they weigh in on what you "should" do with your life. Your manager sees you perform well in some part of your job and he says you "should" do more of it. Quickly he comes to rely on you for it, and since you're a responsible person, you now feel you "should" do it because he wants you to do it. And then he dangles a promotion in front of you, which you feel you "should" take because, after all, he's been so supportive of you. And besides, this promotion brings with it more money and a bigger title, so of course you "should" take it, shouldn't you?

Yes, the world is full of "shoulds." And some of these "shoulds" are worth listening to. But what happens when all these "shoulds" contradict that small, wise voice inside you calling you to do something else? What happens when the world, even a very well-intended world, is wrong about you? What happens when you feel yourself being pushed in a direction that doesn't fit you? What then should you do?

The film answers this question. Watch it. Enjoy it, and learn what you can from it. It will set you up right for the rest of your career.

After you've watched the film, and want to apply what you've learned to your own life, read the book. The book takes up where the film leaves off. It tells you what you can actually do to identify your strengths and push your world toward them. Here you'll learn how to identify your own strengths and weaknesses, how to pick the right roles that play to your strengths, and how to mold your job so that it shows off the very best of you.

The book isn't all reading. In fact, you'll find three specific tasks the book asks you to do. These tasks won't take much time, but they will teach you what you need to know about *you*. If you're serious about you—about identifying your strengths, choosing the right roles, and succeeding in the roles you choose—then complete these three tasks.

After all, you want success. You want to choose the right career path and then make all the right moves so that you can thrive on this path. You want to take all your yearnings to make a difference, to make a name for yourself, to fulfill your dreams, and turn them into practical strategies for how to make these yearnings come true. You want the world to see and feel and recognize and love and, in the end, benefit from the very best of you. You want all these things.

So watch the film. Read the book. Do the tasks. And when you're done, you'll know the truth about you—you'll know how to take a stand for your strengths and make them work for you. You'll discover your own secret to success.

FIRST REACTIONS

Ewan was a competent trombonist, but he felt his strengths pushing him in a different direction. He listened to the advice of his teacher, and he respected that advice, but in the end he chose to take a stand for his strengths. And he did so responsibly. He didn't just leave his bandmates in the lurch without their lead trombonist. Instead, he actively sought out partners who could complement him. He took it upon himself to find a lasting solution.

What did you think of the film? Ewan's was a simple story, but we packed a lot into those twenty-two minutes. Take a moment to write down your top-of-mind reactions to what you've just seen and heard. What struck a chord with you?

What do you remember most?

In the film we identified the three myths that could pull you off track and pinpointed the three truths you must replace them with. These truths will be the building blocks for your success in life. Look at them, lock them in, and never forget them.

TRUTH #1

As you grow, you become more and more of who you already are.

During your life, your dreams may change, your values may change, and your skills will certainly change. But the core of your personality—how patient you are, how competitive, how organized, how charming—will remain remarkably stable throughout the course of your life.

TRUTH #2

You grow most in your areas of greatest strength.

It sounds odd, but you will improve the most, learn the most, be the most creative, be the most inquisitive, and bounce back the fastest in those areas where you have already shown some natural advantage over everyone else—your strengths. This doesn't mean you should ignore your weaknesses. It just means you'll grow most where you're already strong.

TRUTH #3

A great team player volunteers his strengths to the team most of the time and deliberately partners with people who have different strengths.

Of course, you will occasionally have to step out of your strengths zone and do whatever it takes to help the team. But this isn't the core of teamwork. The core of teamwork is partnering with people whose strengths are different from yours.

**THE BEST ADVICE
YOU'LL EVER GET**

THE BEST ADVICE
YOU'LL EVER GET

I've been blessed in my career. I graduated from college and came to America to pursue my interest in psychology. It was a bold move. I left my home in London and moved to Lincoln, Nebraska, where I had no friends, no family, and little money. Things worked out well. I joined a wonderful organization, the Gallup Organization, and got the chance to learn from one of the truly greats in my field, the late Dr. Donald Clifton. His approach was to push decision making as close to the action as possible, so, from a very young age, I was given significant responsibility. I was asked to lead seminars, write reports for our most important clients, and make decisions about how we should spend our time and money. It was heady stuff for a young man fresh out of college.

I worked hard, met some amazingly supportive people, and over time, was challenged to cultivate my strengths to the nth degree. My seminars grew into speeches in front of thousands of people. My reports became books, four of them now, which have sold more than three million copies and have been translated into twenty-seven different languages. I've shared the stage with presidents, generals, chief executives, and even been recruited to join former secretary of state Colin Powell's committee on leadership and management. It's been a wild ride.

But looking back, I realize how many mistakes I made along the way. I was trained in those three foundational truths, and I knew them by heart, but still I wound up doing some really dumb things. There were times when I lost my way, times when I listened to the "shoulds" of the world more closely than I did to the calling of my strengths inside me. And for stretches of my career, I found myself far off my strengths path, doing things that I was capable of doing but that dragged me down and drained me.

I wish someone had given me career advice. I wish someone had taken me aside and told me, clearly and simply, how the world worked and how I could take control of my path within this world. Of course, I would still have made a few mistakes—we all do, and we can learn from these mistakes. Nonetheless, I wish someone had shown me how to stay on my strengths path so that when the blind will of the world tried to pull me off, I could have fought back.

What follows in this book are the five pieces of advice I wish I'd been given:

THE BEST ADVICE YOU'LL EVER GET

1 **Performance is always the point**

*So don't expect your organization ever to know you
like you do.*

2 **Your strengths aren't what you're good at,
and your weaknesses aren't what you're bad at**

So you'd better find out what your real strengths are.

3 **When it comes to your job, the "What" always trumps
the "Why" and the "Who"**

So always ask: "What will I be paid to do?"

4 **You'll never find the perfect job**

*So every week, for the rest of your life, write your
Strong Week Plan.*

5 **You'll never turn your weaknesses into strengths**

So fess up to your weaknesses, then neutralize them.

PERFORMANCE IS ALWAYS THE POINT 1

So don't expect your organization ever to know you like you do

PERFORMANCE IS
ALWAYS THE POINT

This is blunt, but it's true. And you need to recognize it.

Organizations will recruit you saying, "Our people are our greatest asset." They will tell you that they are looking only for the best and the brightest, that you may be one of them, and that, if you join them, you will have the chance to learn, grow, build a great career, get promoted, and, of course, earn a good living. When organizations say these things to you, they aren't trying to mislead you. They are genuine.

But your organization doesn't care primarily about you and your strengths. If you're lucky, your individual manager will. Your organization, however, has other things on its mind. What your organization cares about most is performance. It cares about getting a job done. It cares about meeting the needs of its customers, serving a mission, and making a profit.

And there's nothing wrong with this. This is the way it should be. Organizations are built to serve a specific purpose. This purpose can be financial—"Our mission is to provide an excellent return to our shareholders." Or it can be charitable—"Our mission is to design water purification systems for poor communities around the world." Or it can be a combination of the two—"Our mission is to sell water purification systems for a little more than it takes to make them, and so give a profit to our shareholders."

But whichever, performance is the point of the organization.

It's important to remember that you and your strengths are *not* the point. Your organization was *not* built to help you identify your strengths and show them off to the rest of the world. Sure, your strengths can be useful to the organization's end. But never forget that you are a means to its end. And its desired end is performance.

DON'T EXPECT YOUR ORGANIZATION EVER TO KNOW YOU LIKE YOU DO

What this means is that the organization you work for won't ever truly know you. It'll know what you get done. It'll measure your performance. It'll give you a rating, a title, and maybe even a career ladder for you to climb. But it'll never really know your strengths, or your weaknesses, or what triggers you, or how you learn, or which situations bring out the best in you. And so it is just as likely to put you into a job that truly fits you as it is to push you into a job that isn't right for you at all but simply needs to get done. The organization will start with the performance it wants—a job that needs to get done—and then it'll work backward into you.

Again, to be clear, your organization isn't wrongheaded to think this way, but this is, in the end, why so many people wind up in a job where they are mediocre, unhappy, or both.

Of course, the best way to avoid this is to take yourself seriously from the get-go. Since your organization will never truly know you, it's going to fall to you to know yourself well enough to stay on your strengths path. It's going to fall to you to figure out how to use your strengths to drive the performance your organization wants. This way everyone will win—your organization gets the performance it wants, and you'll get to succeed by playing to your strengths.

How can you do this?

START BY TAKING YOUR INTERESTS SERIOUSLY

You've been raised to believe that other people know you better than you know yourself. At school, you were given grades to tell you what your strengths and weaknesses were. You've taken tests to reveal what career path you should take. Parents, teachers, career counselors, managers—they've all weighed in on what you should do with your life.

All of these people mean well. And sure, over time you are going to meet some wonderful people who inspire you, offer you opportunities, and teach you something about the world and about yourself.

But always remember: you are the greatest teacher about you and your strengths.

During the course of your career, you'll come to discover this. You'll make a misstep into a role that offers you more money or a bigger title but requires you to have strengths you lack, or you'll work for a manager who just doesn't understand you at all, and with each new experience, each step or misstep, you'll come to realize that you are the person you should have listened to most closely all along. Experience will, over time, teach you just how well you know your own strengths.

But don't rely on experience. Start looking now. And the best place to start is with your *interests*. Your interests are a very good clue to your strengths. Your interests aren't random. You're not intrigued by one thing one day and another thing the next. Sure, your interests do change and develop as you get older, but they aren't random. Your interests are part of a pattern inside you. They are the first sign of some force inside you trying to get out, something important in you that needs to be understood and expressed.

They may not tell you right away what job you should have. (Although sometimes they do—my sister danced before she could walk; Matt Damon and Ben Affleck used to discuss their latest scripts in their middle school cafeteria; Sean "P. Diddy" Combs promoted his first concert at seventeen.) Nonetheless, they are worth paying attention to. Wisdom, it is said, can be found in what you choose to overlook. In this sense, your interests are wise. They cause you to overlook a bunch of other stuff and zero in on something specific.

You want to know what you are interests are? Take a moment to look back over your life and ask yourself some questions. Start with what you've done.

- Have you ever held a job?
- Was it just for the money, or did it spark something in you?
- Was there any part of the job that really intrigued you?
- Was there any part of the job you can honestly say you loved?

Think a minute and then write it down:

_____

_____

_____

_____

_____

Okay, now let's move on to your hobbies.

- Do you have any hobbies or special interests?
- Have you ever joined a club or group (other than to pad your résumé) and found yourself actually looking forward to going every week?
- What was it?

_____

_____

_____

_____

_____

Okay, now on to reading.

- What were the last two books you read?
- When you walk past a newsstand, which two magazines do you always buy?
- When you read these magazines, do you find yourself drawn to certain kinds of articles or certain subjects? Which ones?
- When surfing the Web, which sites are you drawn to?
- Which articles do you tend to read online?

Finally, look at the people in your life. Take a moment to think about your friends and close colleagues.

- What kinds of people do you find yourself drawn to?
- What words would you use to describe these people?

Okay, now look at what you've written down. Scan your answers and try to pick out a couple of interests, a couple of things you are consistently drawn to. It might not be easy because you've probably captured quite a lot, but push yourself to be selective. Choose three things, or subjects, or types of people that you know in your heart are deeply seated interests of yours. And then write them down.

MY INTERESTS

1

2

3

Obviously I don't know what you've written, but it's
guaranteed that no one else in the world wrote exactly what
you did. Your interests are the first and most obvious sign
that you are not the same as everyone else. And so, to live
a strong, successful life, your interests are the first thing
you must take seriously.

A great many people don't. They are quick to discount their
interests. They make mental trade-offs with themselves,
saying things like, "I am really interested in teaching, but I
want to make a lot of money first. So I'll go into banking,
work hard for ten years, and then give it all up and go teach."
Or, "I'm interested in art, but I can't make a living at it. So I'll
go get a real job and then do my art on nights and weekends."

In almost every instance these trades are bad trades. They
force you to do something almost impossible: put your real
personality on hold and then try to bring it back to life at
some point in the future.

The problem is that while you're waiting for that future to
arrive, you spend hour upon hour, for years at a time, doing

things that don't interest you. And this takes its toll. Even if you manage to perform well in this "non-you" role, it still takes its toll. Your motivation suffers. Your confidence suffers. Your reputation suffers. Interesting people attract others, and with your interests disengaged from your work, you become less attractive, less fun to be around, less energetic. You slowly lose your sense of who you are and what you can do. And so when that "future" finally arrives, you aren't the same person anymore. You've lost yourself along the way.

Don't let this happen to you. Don't make this trade. Look closely at your interests and take them seriously. Start pushing your life toward them now.

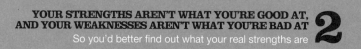

**YOUR STRENGTHS AREN'T WHAT YOU'RE GOOD AT,
AND YOUR WEAKNESSES AREN'T WHAT YOU'RE BAD AT**

So you'd better find out what your real strengths are

YOUR STRENGTHS AREN'T WHAT YOU'RE GOOD AT, AND YOUR WEAKNESSES AREN'T WHAT YOU'RE BAD AT

Your interests are a good place to start, but clearly there's more to your strengths than just interests. To push your life toward your strengths, you have to be able to describe exactly what they are. Most people struggle with this. When you ask people in job interviews, "What are your strengths?" their answers tend to be broad, things like, "I like working with people" or, "I like to be challenged."

A strength as broad as this isn't much help to anyone— you, your interviewer, or your boss. You say you like working with people. Okay, well, what exactly are you doing with the people? Are you selling to them? Or serving them? Or inspiring them? Or charming them? Or teaching them?

And besides, which kinds of people are we talking about here? Do you like working with *all* people? Or is it a certain kind of person? Customers, perhaps. Or people you don't know. Or only people you know well. Or patients. Or students. Or only new employees.

To push your life and your job toward your strengths, you have to be specific about exactly which activities are your strengths.

This can be hard to do, because you've been raised to believe—as we've all been raised to believe—that your strengths are what you're good at and your weaknesses are what you are bad at. But this "truth" falls apart when you look at it even a little closely. Of course, "something you're good at" is a fine place to start when you try to identify your strengths. But it's only the start. Don't you have some things that you're good at, but they bore you, drain you, or frustrate you? You are certainly capable of doing them, and because you're capable of doing them, people keep asking you to do them—in fact, they come to rely on you to do them—but if you never had to do those things again it would be too soon.

What do you call activities like that?

As I said in the film, I once knew a guy who was an amazing swimmer but would get crushing migraines before every swimming competition. I'm sure you know people like this: the young tennis superstar who just can't seem to get excited about beating her opponent; the kid with the soloist voice who almost faints at the thought of singing solo in public; the wizard at math who's certainly capable of solving the most complicated equations but who's bored to tears while he does it.

Well, what do you call that? Something you've been blessed with lots of ability to do well but cursed with no appetite for it. Something you're brilliant at, but that leaves you cold—or in my friend's case, broken down.

You call that a *weakness*. A weakness is any activity that leaves you feeling weaker after you do it. It doesn't matter how good you are at it or how much money you make doing it, if doing it drains you of energy, you'd be crazy to build your career around it.

Of course, a strength is the opposite. A strength—your strengths—are any activities that *make you feel strong*. To discover your strengths, you must look beyond "what you're good at" and pay really close attention to what you're feeling before, during, and after an activity. Your feelings will tell you what your strengths are.

If, *before* you do something, you find yourself actually looking forward to doing it, it may be a strength.

If, *while* you're doing something, you feel focused, in the zone, with time whipping by really quickly, it may be a strength.

If, *after* you're done, you feel fulfilled, it may be a strength.

Not fulfilled as in, "I'm so happy that's over." But fulfilled as in, "That really gave me a kick." You may be tired, but you're not drained. Instead you feel the opposite of drained. You feel filled up.

Your strengths are the specific activities that *make you feel strong*.

Here's a simple way to remember what to look for when trying to spot your strengths:

S = SUCCESS

If you have some *success* at the activity, it may be a strength.

I = INSTINCT

If, before you do it, you find yourself *instinctively* looking forward to doing it, it may be strength.

G = GROWTH

If, while you're doing it, you find yourself easily able to concentrate (your synapses firing, your brain literally *growing*), it may be a strength.

N = NEEDS

If, after you've done it, it feels like it fulfills a *need* of yours, it may be a strength.

YOU'D BETTER FIND OUT
WHAT YOUR REAL STRENGTHS ARE

You don't need anyone else to tell you what your strengths are. All you need is to pay attention to how you feel before, during, and after you do something. All you need is a regular week of your life.

And a ReMemo pad.

You can find your ReMemo pad in the back of this book. Take it out and look at it. You'll see that it's a notepad of twenty-four blue pages with "I Loved It" written at the top. Flip it around and you'll see it's now twenty-four black pages with "I Loathed It" at the top.

To identify what your real strengths are, here's what you have to do.

Carry this notepad around with you for a week. Anytime you feel yourself looking forward to doing something, scribble down on one of the blue cards the activity you're looking forward to.

Anytime you find yourself in the zone, time going by quickly, then stop and scribble down on one of the blue cards what you are doing.

Anytime you find yourself at the end feeling jazzed and energized, scribble down what you just did.

Don't wait until the end of the day, or the end of the week, and then try to remember what you did. You'll wind up with something too broad like, "I felt strong working with people." Or, "I felt strong when I was challenged." Just scribble down exactly what you are doing right when you are doing it.

And don't judge what you're writing and try to change it to make it sound better. Just write down what you were doing. If you found yourself "in the zone" while watching a movie, then fine, write that down. If you felt fulfilled after color-coding your sock drawer, then fine, write that down. No matter what you were doing, if you felt strong before, during, or after doing it, then write it down on one of the blue cards. (Leave the black cards for another week.)

And above all, make sure you are capturing things that *you* are doing, not things that are being done to you. So, for example, don't write down, "I felt strong when my boss praised me." Or, "I felt strong when people liked my ideas." Instead make sure you write down only things that *you* are doing, such as, "I felt strong when I persuaded my boss to support my idea" or, "I felt strong when I found the best flight rates for my spring vacation."

And then, when the week is over, tear out all the blue cards you've written on. Lay them out. There are probably fifteen to twenty cards lying in front of you. Flip through them. Look at each card closely. These fifteen to twenty activities are the best of your week, the high points. Some of them won't surprise you at all. Some of them will—"Did I really get jazzed helping my friend paint his new apartment?" But what's certain is that no one has quite the same things written on their blue cards as you do. Your fifteen to twenty cards are you. Uniquely you. Uniquely the best of you. These blue cards hold the key to your strengths.

Flip through them one more time, and pick out one where

you're absolutely certain you felt strong before, during, and after you were doing it.

I have no idea what you wrote on the card, but what I do know for certain is that when you read it you won't struggle to remember what it was. Instead, when you read it, you will immediately be transported back to that exact moment when you felt compelled to take out the ReMemo pad and write down what you were doing. So, as an example, if for some reason you wrote on your card: "I felt strong when I painted my friend's new apartment," rereading the card will bring you right back there. Suddenly you can smell the paint. You can see the spattering on your T-shirt. You can hear the scrape of the stepladder as you pulled it across the floor. This is your life. These are your emotions. When you recall them, every sense switches back on, and you're back in the moment.

To capture one of your strengths, use this blue card to come up with a clear Strength Statement. A Strength Statement begins with the phrase "I feel strong when . . ." and then continues with you describing an activity. This activity has to be specific enough to give you an emotional punch when you read it, but it has to be general enough for you to use in a lot of different situations—to continue with our example, obviously you don't need to be painting your friend's apartment every week.

Your goal should be to write three clear Strength Statements. You will need these three Strength Statements to help you find the right job and to succeed in this job once you're in it. For now, just try to write one. One really good one. A statement that when you read it, it gives you strength. It creates in you the same kind of strong emotions that pushed you to scribble in the ReMemo pad in the first place.

Here's how you do it.

First, *pick a verb*. Look at your blue card. What were you actually *doing* when you wrote it down? Sticking with the example of painting your friend's apartment, what was it exactly that gave you a kick? Was it that you were painting? Is painting the verb? "I feel strong when I *paint* . . ." Does this feel right when you read it?

Or was the painting irrelevant? Perhaps it wasn't the painting. After all, you've got another blue card here where you wrote, "I felt strong when I helped my friend lay tile in his bathroom."

So maybe it wasn't the painting. It was the helping. What gave you a kick was the fact you were *helping* your friend. Try that. "I feel strong when I *help* . . ." Does this feel right when you read it?

You get the point. Look at your blue card and pick the verb.

Second, *drill down* to specifics. Let's say you picked the verb *help*. All right, now ask yourself, does it matter who you are helping? Of course it does. You don't feel strong when you help anybody, anytime, anywhere. It's more specific than that. Maybe it's that you like helping people you care about do something they would really struggle to do without you. If so, then your Strength Statement will read: "I feel strong when I help my close friends and family do things they can't do by themselves."

Or maybe it's that you are really good at doing home improvement work, and what gives you a kick is when people, any people, ask you to do anything you are an expert in. If so, your Strength Statement will read: "I feel strong when I help people do things where I know I excel."

Again, you get the point.

So look at your blue card, and now drill down. Get specific. What is it about the activity that drove you to write it down in the first place? What *matters* about the activity?

Think for a minute, and then try to write your first Strength Statement:

"I feel strong when..."

Last, *feel it.* Read your Strength Statement back to yourself. It should give you an emotional jolt. Strong feelings pushed you to write it down on the blue card in the first place. You should feel strong feelings again when you read the Strength Statement you created from it. You read the statement and you feel, "Yes! That's right! That's true! That's me!" Your body language changes. You find yourself smiling. You sit up a little straighter. You feel stronger, more powerful, in your sweet spot. You start to look forward to when you can do it again.

If you feel all these things, great. You've written your first Strength Statement.

Now go back to your pile of blue cards. Choose two more that leap out at you. Then, with each, pick a verb, drill down to the specifics, and write two more Strength Statements. You'll find a place to write these down on page 55.

These three Strength Statements are your map. They do all the things a map does for you. They tell you which direction you should take next—should you take this job or that job?

They show someone else where you are—in a job interview, say, when you're asked about your strengths, you'll now be able to give three specific, vivid examples, and because they come directly from your own life you'll be able to speak about them with power. You'll be persuasive and memorable precisely because your descriptions of your strengths are so vivid, and so heartfelt.

They can help you refocus and find a new way forward when an obstacle gets in your way.

They can be used to help your manager see your best route, your "path of least resistance" toward the performance she wants from you.

On the flip side, without your Strength Statements, you'll be without your map. And you'll get lost.

By the way, don't judge what you write and try to make it "sound" better. Just to show you that what matters is how the activity made you *feel*, not how "good" it sounds, the prize for the most bizarre blue card goes to the guy who'd written on one of his: "I felt strong when I got myself punched in the face."

He was in one of my seminars, and he looked like a regular guy. Black suit. Button-down shirt. Computer open on the table in front of him. Except the white of his left eye was red from burst blood vessels. Clearly someone had indeed punched him in the face in the last week.

But there he was, sitting up straight, smiling, reading his card to all of us: "I felt strong when I got myself punched in the face."

"Are you sure?" I asked.

"Yeah," he replied, "it felt great when it happened. I was fulfilled afterward. And even now, now that I'm thinking about it again, it feels so good it almost gives me goosebumps."

The room got pretty quiet.

"Er, why?"

"Because I do martial arts in my spare time, and last week, during a sparring match, this guy just nailed me. And right then and there, I learned you should never, ever lead with your head. I'd been told this many times, but my problem is that I can't learn by being told something. And I can't learn by writing it down. I learn only by doing. By trial and error. I'd sort of always been aware that this is how I learned, but when that guy punched me, I suddenly got it, boom, flashes of light going off in my head. I suddenly learned how I learned."

And so from this weird blue card, and from his drill down to the specifics of it, came the following Strength Statement:

"I feel strong whenever I put myself in high-pressure situations and force myself to learn what I need to do to win."

This Strength Statement won't help you. But it will help him. It'll help him put himself in exactly the right kind of situations where he can succeed.

Yours will do the same for you.

1 **STRENGTH STATEMENT**
Number one

I feel strong when...

2 **STRENGTH STATEMENT**
Number two

I feel strong when...

3 **STRENGTH STATEMENT**
Number three

I feel strong when...

WHEN IT COMES TO YOUR JOB, THE "WHAT" ALWAYS TRUMPS THE "WHY" AND THE "WHO"

So always ask: "What will I be paid to do?"

3

WHEN IT COMES TO YOUR JOB, THE "WHAT" ALWAYS TRUMPS THE "WHY" AND THE "WHO"

Newton's law of gravity says that what goes up must come down.

Moore's law of computing says that computer chips will double in processing power every eighteen months.

Buckingham's law of careers says that, in the end, the "What" always trumps the "Why" and the "Who."

People tend to take a job because of the "Why"—"I'm joining the Peace Corps to help the disadvantaged" or, "I'm going into politics to make a difference" or, "I'm going into sales to make a lot of money."

They stay in a job because of the relationships they build, because of "Who" they work with—"I like my colleagues. They know me. They expect things of me. I don't want to let them down."

But then, as time drags on, they gradually become aware that "What" they are actually doing isn't what they want to be doing. They ReMemo and, even though they love the purpose of their work and like the people they work with, they finish their week with very few blue cards. The actual activities of their job do not play to their strengths. And so they quit.

People join because of the "Why." They stay because of the "Who." And, in the end, they quit because of the "What."

Here are a few examples of Buckingham's law at work:

The flight attendant applies to flight attendant school because she likes the idea of travel—the purpose of the business, the *why* of it intrigues her. She sticks with the job because, over time, she gets to be friends with her fellow flight attendants—she likes *who* she works with. And she quits because finally, at forty, she realizes that she is drained by *what* a flight attendant is actually paid to do—namely, win over planefuls of grumpy passengers.

The nurse trains to be a nurse because her mother told her she is a nurturing person and she doesn't want to disappoint her mother—not disappointing her mother, that's her "why." She stays on as a nurse because she feels a bond with the other nurses in her neonatal unit. They know and trust one another. Then, ten years later, she admits to herself that what nurses actually do—stop the bleeding, administer the medications, check the medications, record the patient's response, and do it all again tomorrow with the endless supply of sick people— bores her. It doesn't let her create anything. And that's what she's always wanted to do: create something. More specifically, create something for people to eat. So she enrolls in culinary night school, earns her qualification, applies for a job running a cafeteria in a corporate office, gets it, and quits nursing. Finally, she feels she's living the life she was always supposed to live.

The English teacher jumps on the opportunity to design
a new curriculum for the entire school district—her "why"
is that it will look good on her résumé and pay her more.
And she plugs away at it because she is a responsible
person who feels that the colleagues on the design team
have come to rely on her. But after three years, she takes
stock: "I don't want to design curriculum," she confesses
to herself. "What I want to do is meet my sixth graders
in the morning, ask them what books they read over the
weekend, read them myself, and then lead a discussion
about the books in class. That's what I really want to do at
work." She resigns from the design curriculum committee
and refocuses her life on teaching real students in a real
classroom.

The young salesman applies at a pharmaceutical
organization to become a junior sales rep—he's always been
good at sales and he knows that salespeople can make
good money. He stays because he respects his boss and
makes friends with many of his clients. But one morning he
wakes up and realizes that a pharmaceutical sales rep never
gets to close a sale. All he can ever hope to do is make a

good enough impression on the doctors he calls on so that at some time in the future they will wind up prescribing more of his drugs than his competitors'. "I'm a salesperson who never gets to sell," he says to himself. And selling, really and truly closing a sale, hearing a yes or turning around a no, is what he wants to be doing. But he's not. So he quits and joins a medical device organization where he has to leave the doctor's office with the actual sales order.

It may take years of confusion and frustration and good intentions, but in the end Buckingham's law always prevails. In the end, the "what" always trumps the "why" and the "who."

So get the "what" right. Get it right, right from the start.

Here's a simple way to do this.

ALWAYS ASK: "WHAT WILL I BE PAID TO DO?"

It's strange. Organizations know they want performance, but they aren't good at defining what it is. Go to one of those online job posting boards and read a couple of job descriptions. You'll see a job post, and it will tell you the title, the salary, the benefits, and all the necessary experience or qualifications, but it will rarely tell you in simple, plain language what exactly you will be paid to do.

This can cause you big problems. If you aren't careful, you'll wind up applying for jobs or taking on roles that don't fit you, all because no one ever told you what you were actually going to be paid to do.

The job title "stockbroker" is a good example. Lots of people say they want to be stockbrokers. It is, after all, a job that carries with it a good salary and respect in your community. And companies are very clear about what kinds of qualifications you must have in order to become a stockbroker—you must pass your Series 7 and Series 63 tests, for example.

But do you know what a stockbroker is actually paid to do? A stockbroker is paid to call up two hundred strangers a week and ask them for money. One hundred and ninety of these people will say no. Turning around consistent personal rejection, that's the job of a stockbroker. That's what he's paid to do.

You may find this work appealing, or you may not. You may hate this kind of personal rejection, or you may get kind of a kick out of it. But you won't be able to make a decision either way if you don't know what a stockbroker is actually paid to do.

The bottom line is that most job descriptions don't describe the actual job very well.

This means it's up to you to make it clear. Whenever you find yourself interviewing for a new job, push your potential boss to tell you what you're going to be paid to do. Use those exact words: "What will I be paid to do?"

Don't try to ask the question in business-speak, such as, "What results will you expect me to produce?" or, "What performance metrics will be used to judge my performance?" Just put it in plain English:

"What exactly will I be paid to do?"

And then write it down. Write down whatever your potential boss says and believe it. No matter how much you like the job description, or the job title, or the money, you will thrive or fail at this job based on the actual activities of the job. You need to know what you will be doing at 9 a.m. on a regular Thursday morning, or 2 p.m. on an average Monday afternoon. That right there is the job. Look at it full on.

Compare it to your three Strength Statements, and then ask yourself these two questions:

1 **Can I see myself doing these actual activities?**

2 **How can I use my three strengths to get this job done?**

Then make your decision.

YOU'LL NEVER FIND THE PERFECT JOB

So every week, for the rest of your life, write your Strong Week Plan

YOU'LL NEVER FIND THE PERFECT JOB

Think about the most effective person you know. The person who is not only good at her job but also seems happy in her work. She's busy. Hardworking. Engaged. Successful. Other people want to work with her. She always seems to get the best assignments. Things always seem to work out for her.

Do you have someone in mind?

You look at her and think, *You lucky devil. How did you find that job? How did you find a job that fits you so well?*

It's a trick question, because when you look at her closely, you discover that she didn't find this job. She *built* it. She

took a generic job description—check the online posting
boards for a million examples—and then week by week,
she deliberately pushed her time toward those activities
that strengthened her and away from those that didn't.
She pushed and she pushed, her stack of blue cards
growing, until the *best* of her job became *most* of
her job.

She slowly but deliberately rewrote her job description
under her boss's nose.

So should you.

EVERY WEEK, FOR THE REST OF YOUR LIFE,
WRITE YOUR STRONG WEEK PLAN.

This is how things will play out.

First, you'll pinpoint what your interests are.

Then you'll ReMemo and write three Strength Statements
drawn from your own life. Every time you read your three
Strength Statements you'll get a jolt. Your shoulders will

snap back and you'll straighten up, taller, more powerful. Then you'll seek out roles that match your strengths.

Then you'll go to the interview, you'll talk about your strengths vividly, clearly, persuasively, and you'll get the job you want.

And then, when you show up for your first day, you'll start your training and you'll be given a long list of things you're supposed to get done, outcomes you're supposed to achieve. It will be quite overwhelming, and for the first couple of weeks your brain time will be taken up with learning all that you need to learn so that you don't mess up badly enough to get yourself kicked off the team.

A month goes by. Two months. Three months.

You've started to get comfortable with your new role. You've figured out its rhythms, its tricks, even its shortcuts. Sure, you still have a lot to learn, but you've got the basics down. Your boss has told you what you're responsible for, and you've delivered.

Now what?

The chances are you've discovered that the job doesn't fit
you perfectly. There are parts you like and parts you don't.
And someone—a colleague, your manager—will tell you
to suck it up and do what needs to be done. He'll tell you
that you have to pay your dues, and that if you want to get
promoted up to the next level you've got to be prepared to
do whatever it takes to get the job done. He'll tell you you've
got to become well-rounded.

Don't listen to him.

Instead, remember the second truth from the film: *You will
grow the most in your areas of greatest strength.* You will
improve the most, learn the most, be most creative, most
inquisitive, and bounce back fastest in those areas where
you have already shown some natural advantage over
everyone else—your strengths.

It's a competitive world out there. You'll make your greatest,
longest-lasting, most extraordinary, most memorable

contribution when you figure out where you have some natural advantage over everybody else, and then push and push those strengths into play.

Of course your job doesn't fit you perfectly. Nobody's job ever does. Once you realize this, the best thing you can do is start the gradual, week-by-week process of carving the job to fit the best of you. So each week, every week, write a Strong Week Plan. This won't take much time. Ten or fifteen minutes tops. It's just two things you are going to do this week to tip the scales toward your strengths.

I know that there's a lot you have to do on your job, and you have a manager looking over your shoulder making sure you do it. But it doesn't matter what your job is, or who your manager is, over time you'll discover that you have the freedom to slowly change your job to fit your strengths better.

Each week, pick out two things you are going to do to put your strengths into play. One week you'll look for some new way in which your strengths can help the team, and you'll raise your hand and volunteer. One week you'll find a missed opportunity to apply your strengths to help your customers, and you'll take action. One week you'll read an article about how someone like you used her strengths to stand out from the crowd. One week you'll try out a new technique to make one of your strengths even more powerful. One week you'll take a more experienced colleague out to lunch and pick his brain about how he does what he does. One week you'll sign up for a class that'll help you sharpen one of your strengths.

That's all your Strong Week Plan is: two things you are going to commit to this week that will put your strengths into play. Each week you are going to say to yourself, "I am not going to let the week go by without doing these two things."

And every time you do this, you'll talk to your manager about it in terms of how it will help the team succeed. You'll go to him and say: "I've been thinking about ways I can be more productive, so would it be okay if I . . ." And some weeks he'll turn you down. But there'll be many weeks where he'll say, "Why not? Let's try it and see if it helps the team. Go for it."

And gradually, week by week, three things will happen.

First, your job will change—your job description will look like it was written specifically for you. You'll start to *feel* different. You'll not only get your work done more effectively, but you'll also get the energy you need to power through some of the other stuff in your job that bores you or frustrates you.

Second, you'll gain a reputation—the right kind of reputation, the "he's got initiative" kind, the "he keeps searching for better ways" kind, the "he's a top performer" kind.

And third, people will look at you and think, *You lucky devil. How did you find that job? How did you find a job that fits you so well?*

And you'll know the answer. You didn't find it. You built it. A little each week, and a lot over time.

YOU'LL NEVER TURN YOUR WEAKNESSES INTO STRENGTHS

What about all the other stuff? What about all the activities in your job that bore you, or frustrate you, or that you struggle with? What about your weaknesses?

Obviously, you can't just ignore them and hope they go away. Down that road lies the worst kind of reputation, poor performance, and in the end, no job.

So what are you going to do with your weaknesses? This is a question every sports superstar has to come to grips with. Shaquille O'Neal still had to make free throws. Tiger Woods, eighty-third on the PGA Tour in sand saves, still had to get himself out of a bunker a couple of times a round.

David Beckham couldn't just bend free kicks around the
wall into the back of the net the whole game. He had to
control the ball and dribble past a defender once in a while.
Tom Brady, not blessed with a cannon arm—which is why
he wasn't picked until the sixth round of the draft—still
occasionally had to hook up with a wide receiver
forty yards downfield.

Everyone has weaknesses. And everyone has to deal
with them.

You're weakened by dealing with expense reports?

Or by making presentations?

Or by memorizing product details?

Or by working as part of a team?

Or by sitting in meetings?

Or by charming people?

Well, sorry to say, but that's the way life is. You're not perfect. You have weaknesses, and no matter how carefully you push your world toward your strengths, you're still going to have to deal with, and deal well with, your weaknesses.

Annoyingly, the people you work with won't ever really understand that your weakness is, in fact, a weakness. Your weakness, you see, isn't the same as their weakness. And since they don't struggle with it, they find it really hard to imagine why you struggle with it. For example, because they happen to like making presentations, they'll never truly understand just how much you hate giving them, which will lead them to say things like: "If you just worked at it and practiced it, you could turn that weakness into a strength."

But they're wrong. Remember the first truth from the film: **As you grow, you become more and more of who you already are.** This means that what weakens you now (and what strengthens you) will probably weaken you just as much twenty years from now. If, today, you feel weakened by dealing with expense reports, or by making presentations, or by memorizing product details, or by working as part of a team, or by sitting in meetings, or by charming people, the chances are that you'll feel the same way when you're ninety.

So what are you going to do? How can you excel at your job while not desperately trying to turn your weaknesses into strengths?

FESS UP TO YOUR WEAKNESSES, THEN NEUTRALIZE THEM

Take out your ReMemo pad again and carry it around with you for another week. But this time, don't write anything on the blue cards. Instead, focus on the black cards. If, before you do something, you find yourself wishing someone else would do it, write it down. If, while you're doing something, you struggle to concentrate, your mind wandering, wishing it were over and done with, then write it down. If you finish something and you find yourself thinking, *Thank God that's over. I hope I never have to do that again,* write it down.

By the end of the week, you'll have a little stack of black

cards. Psychologists call these "negative emotional reactions." Regular people call them a grind, a bore, a pain, a "I wish I could hand this off to the new guy."

From now on, you should call them what they really are: your weaknesses. Your weaknesses aren't just things you're bad at—in fact, as my swimmer friend found out, sometimes you might actually be quite good at them. *Your weaknesses are those activities that weaken you.*

To succeed in life, you need to fess up to them. No one else wrote those black cards. You wrote them. You may wish you hadn't—I know my swimmer friend wished he loved swimming laps—but you *did* write them. Other people may tell you that you *should* like them, or that to get promoted you *have* to like them, but you know the real story. You know you carried your ReMemo pad around with you, and these specific activities ended up on your black cards.

To thrive in life, you must understand your weaknesses so clearly that they never trip you up. So look at your pile of black cards and do exactly what you did with your blues.

Flip through the pile and take out the black card that creates in you the strongest negative emotional reaction.

Then pick the right verb, drill down to the specifics of what you were doing, and write out your first Weakness Statement. (On page 86 you'll find a place to capture your three Weakness Statements.)

"I feel weak (bored, drained) when..."

_____

_____

_____

_____

_____

Read it back to yourself.

It doesn't feel very good. But there it is. Drawn from your own life. Written in your own handwriting. Your weakness.

Remember, as you did with your Strength Statements, your Weakness Statement must be an activity *you* are doing.

Don't write down feelings you have when other people do things to you. For example, don't write down, "I feel weak when my coworkers ignore me during a meeting." In this example, your coworkers are the ones doing. Of course it doesn't feel good to be ignored, but this isn't a weakness of yours. Your weakness is something *you do* that makes you feel weak, bored, or drained. "I feel weak when I work with loners who don't like to collaborate." That's a proper weakness because it is something you are doing.

Why do I make this point so strongly?

Because if your weakness is something *you* do, then it's something *you* can do something about.

THE TRUTH ABOUT YOU
YOUR SECRET TO SUCCESS

 1 WEAKNESS STATEMENT
Number one

I feel weak (drained, bored) when...

2 WEAKNESS STATEMENT
Number two

I feel weak (drained, bored) when...

3 WEAKNESS STATEMENT
Number three

I feel weak (drained, bored) when...

So what are you going to do about it? What can you do to neutralize these weaknesses of yours? Well, you may never turn them into strengths, but you can, and you must deal with them. Here are four tactics to neutralize your weaknesses:

STOP DOING IT

First, just stop doing it and see if anyone cares.
This is the riskiest tactic, but try it. Companies are very good at starting things and terrible at stopping them.
A manager will set up her own systems, meetings, processes, and then she'll move on, and a new manager will show up with his own particular ways of doing things, but somehow the old systems, meetings, and processes will keep going, like 1960s satellites shot up into space, once useful, now out of date, but still circling above your head, space waste.

Some of what ended up on your black cards will be space waste. So just stop doing it, and see if anyone notices. I'm not saying this will work every time, but before you try anything else, try this. It's worth a shot.

PARTNER UP

Second, partner up with someone else. Seek out someone who is strengthened by the very thing that weakens you. Remember the Warren Buffet example from the film? A few years ago Warren Buffett did something bizarre: he gave away $31 billion to the Bill and Melinda Gates Foundation. During a press conference someone asked him, "Why did you do it? Why did you give away your entire fortune to someone else's charity?"

His answer: "Because charity bores me."

Who says this? Some of us may occasionally think this, but who actually comes right out and says this? It's like saying, "Squeezing one more dollar out of my companies is fun for me. But helping underprivileged kids around the world? Big yawn." Who says this?!

I know you're not that worried about the social pressures on a billionaire, but there are social pressures. And one of them is that, after you've banked your first billion, you're

---

supposed to have a charitable cause to which you will give some of your fortune. Well, what Buffett was saying was, "You know what? I'm cause-less. Cause-less in paradise, that's me."

That would be like you coming out and saying, "You know what? I don't like being responsible for other people's work. I know I am supposed to want to be a manager, and get promoted, but I just don't like being responsible for what other people do. All that really gives me a kick is being responsible for my own work."

It takes a self-confident, self-aware person to be able to stand up and fess up to who he really is.

Of course, when Buffett said he was bored by charity work, he wasn't saying it was stupid work. He was saying something much smarter. He was saying, "I so respect the work of charity that it can't be left up to me."

You should do the same. Look hard at your Weakness Statements and then see if there is anyone around you who you can team up with. See if there is someone you work with who is strengthened by the very activities that weaken you. Not because you disrespect the activities, but because you so respect them you know they can't be left up to a person like you.

SHARPEN YOUR STRENGTHS

Third, keep sharpening your strengths and make them so powerful that they render your weaknesses irrelevant. Tiger Woods did this. Compared to his peers, he's weak at getting his ball out of a bunker. His tactic: take his greatest strength—his swing—and make it so solid, so reliable, so accurate that he rarely if ever hits his ball into a bunker. Who needs to excel at getting out of a bunker when you're hardly ever in one?

Tom Brady did this. Brady holds the ball very tightly, which makes his passes exceptionally accurate, but it also prevents him from throwing the ball as far as other quarterbacks like John Elway, Brett Favre, or Brady's predecessor at New England, Drew Bledsoe. Rather than try to transform him into someone he wasn't, his coaches built their game plan around a series of short passing plays that would demand, and capitalize on, Brady's awesome accuracy. When he took over from Bledsoe as the Patriots starting quarterback, Brady threw a record 162 passes in a row without an interception.

David Beckham did this. He developed such strength and accuracy in his passing that he no longer needed to dribble past the defenders in front of him. He made the defender irrelevant by firing sixty-yard passes to his teammate on the opposite side of the field.

You could do this too.

LOOK AT YOUR WEAKNESS THROUGH ONE OF YOUR STRENGTHS

Finally, try looking at your weakness from the perspective of one of your strengths. This is an incredibly effective strategy. Rudy Giuliani, the former mayor of New York City, had a weakness for public speaking. As an attorney, he was good at preparing legal cases to prosecute criminals and was also effective at arguing his cases in court. But as mayor, he struggled with standing behind a lectern and giving a speech to a room full of people. Which was a problem, because the mayor of New York City has to do a lot of this.

So he worked at it. He read Winston Churchill's speeches, he hired a speech coach, and he even sneaked into an empty theatre on 92nd Street to practice his speaking style on a real stage. But no matter how hard he tried, he still struggled. He came across as stiff and stilted.

Until, during one of his late-night practice sessions, his speech coach asked him: "When you think about talking to people, is there any part of it you actually look forward to?"

"I like arguing," Giuliani replied. "I like taking a question and then making my case for why my answer is the best answer."

His coach thought for a moment. "You love arguing. Okay. So turn every speech into an argument. Come out from behind the lectern, leave your notes behind, take questions from the crowd, and then walk around where everyone can see you and make your case. From now on stop making speeches and start winning arguments."

This has been Giuliani's speaking style ever since. Whenever he has to speak, he makes a couple of short remarks from behind the lectern, and then he marches out in front, takes questions, and argues his case. No longer stiff, he comes across as comfortable, powerful, authoritative, exactly what a leader should be. He took his weakness— public speaking. He looked at it from the perspective of his strength—arguing. And he neutralized it.

And, oh by the way, he has also gradually become better and better at doing regular public speaking. You'll find this too. You'll find that when you fall back on one of your strengths, it has a side effect of helping you with your weakness.

Take Shaquille O'Neal as an example. He had a weakness in his game, didn't he? Free throws. When he graduated from Louisiana State, he joined the Orlando Magic and they noticed that, although he dominated under the basket, his free throw percentage was far below 50 percent. And so they told him to work on it. It was hurting the team, they told him. They showed him how to hold the ball differently and throw it so that it would have more of an arc to it. They told him to get into a rhythm where he would bounce the ball a set number of times before attempting each throw.

He practiced and he practiced.

And though he got to be a very good player, his free throw percentage didn't move much at all.

Frustrated with the fact that the Orlando Magic weren't winning championships, Shaq had himself traded to the Los Angeles Lakers. Here he got to work with one of the best basketball coaches in the history of the game, Phil Jackson.

Coach Jackson completely changed Shaq's practice routine. "From now on," he said, "we will spend only an hour a day on free throws. The rest of the time we will work on your play under the basket, your play in the paint."

Shaq was confused. "Why?" he asked. "I'm already one of the best centers in the league."

"Because you could be the best center ever to play the game," replied Jackson. "But you're not. Yet."

So Shaq refined and perfected his play as a center, and the results were extraordinary. Not only did he win the individual scoring title three years in a row, but, more importantly, the LA Lakers won the NBA title three years in a row.

And, oh by the way, during this three-year run, Shaq's free throw percentage jumped twenty points. Sure, he went from being a terrible free thrower to one who was merely really bad, so it's not like he turned his weakness into a strength. Just like Giuliani is still no Churchill when it comes to making a world-changing speech. But nonetheless, the surprising lesson to draw from these guys is that everyone has As and everyone has Fs, and that one of the best ways to net slight improvement in the Fs is by concentrating on the As.

ONE LAST TACTIC

There is one last tactic for dealing with your weakness. If you've tried all the others and they haven't worked—you can't stop doing it, you can't find a teammate to lean on, you can't overpower it with a strength and make it irrelevant, looking at it from the perspective of one of your strengths hasn't helped—then there's only one tactic left: suck it up and do it.

The most successful people play to their strengths *most* of the time, not *all* of the time. Even if you push each week to play to your strengths, you are always going to have some activities on your job that weaken you, some activities that you don't look forward to, that bore you while you're doing them, and that you hope never to do again when you're finally finished.

If you can get your weaknesses down to 25 percent of your day—that's a little more than two hours a day—then you will have plenty of time left over to flex your strength muscles and show the world just how effective you can be.

So suck it up. Recognize that what weakens you is only a small part of your job, and then devote the rest of your time to getting better and better at those things where you have some unfair, natural advantage over everybody else— your strengths.

WARNING!

As you march along your strengths path, you will meet many people along the way who will feel compelled to offer direction. Some of this direction will prove useful. But some of it will be actively dangerous. It will sound good, and it will surely be well intended, but it will hurt you.

Here are five directions that will hurt you. Whenever you hear them, nod your head, smile politely, and then run as fast as you can the other way.

FIVE THINGS THAT SOUND RIGHT BUT AREN'T

1 "Always treat people as you would like to be treated."

2 "There is no I in team."

3 "You should work on your weaknesses."

4 "Push yourself beyond your comfort zone."

5 "Your greatest strength is also your greatest weakness."

1 **"Always treat people as you would like to be treated."**

This is commonly called the Golden Rule.

Break it every day. It is based on the principle that other people would like to be treated the way you would like to be treated.

They don't. They want to be treated the way *they* like to be treated. And the way they want to be treated is not necessarily the way you do.

You want to know how a person likes to be treated? Ask to see his three Strength Statements and his three Weakness Statements. How else will you discover that your mild-mannered coworker learns best by being punched in the face?

2 "There is no I in team."

Your manager will normally say this when she's trying to make you realize that the team's performance is more important than your individual performance, and that a good team member puts aside his strengths and does whatever it takes to help the team.

This isn't true. What we, your teammates, need to know from you is what your strengths are, where your shoulders are broadest, and when the pressure is on, what plays we can count on you to run.

Of course, sometimes we, your teammates, will need you to chip in and do something that doesn't quite fit your strengths. But most of the time, we don't want you to do this. Most of the time, we want you to know yourself well enough to tell us where we can count on you. The best teams have lots of I's in them, lots of individuals who know their strengths clearly and volunteer these strengths to the team.

Always remember: the best teams are not made up of lots of well-rounded people all playing every role equally well. Instead, as I said in the film, the best teams are made up of lots of sharp people who have deliberately partnered up with other people who are sharp where they are blunt. And so the best *teams* are well-rounded precisely because each individual on the team *isn't*.

3 **"You should work on your weaknesses."**

No, you shouldn't.

Working on your weaknesses will drag you down and, at best, will lead to small improvements. Instead, you should call your weaknesses what they really are, "things that weaken you," and then you should figure out ways to manage around them.

Your weaknesses are not "areas for development" or "areas of opportunity." They are areas of *least* opportunity. They are your kryptonite. They sap your strengths. So don't work on them. Figure out creative ways to neutralize them. That's what the most successful people do.

4 "Push yourself beyond your comfort zone."

This one sounds right because, of course, you *should* keep learning and growing and experimenting throughout your career. But it's not true. It leads people such as Michael Jordan to try their hand at professional baseball.

Instead, you should push yourself *within* your comfort zone.

Your strengths are your comfort zone. You can see what your comfort zone is by flicking through your blue cards. These blue cards, your strengths, are not only activities that strengthen you, but they are also activities where you have the greatest *capacity* to learn and grow. So if you are going to push yourself—and you should—then push yourself to get better and better at expressing what's on those blue cards.

5 **"Your greatest strength is also your greatest weakness."**

This one misses the point. Your strengths can't also be weaknesses, because what strengthens you can't also weaken you.

What is the point? The point is that your strengths are value neutral. They are a blind force inside you that demands to be expressed. Sometimes your strengths can be expressed productively, and sometimes unproductively. But either way, they are going to come out.

A colleague of mine used to worry her mother because every Sunday she would walk into their pantry and turn every single item on the shelves so that the label was facing out. To her mom it looked like a classic case of perfectionism, of paying an unhealthy amount of attention to detail. The mother even started to worry that her daughter suffered from obsessive-compulsive disorder.

And I suppose it could have played out this way, with the mother becoming increasingly concerned, chiding her daughter to stop, seeking treatment and even medication.

But it didn't play out this way. Instead, her mother chose to see her daughter's craving for order as a strength to be channeled, not a weakness to be fixed. She and her daughter talked about why she felt compelled to rearrange hundreds of items on the pantry shelves every week—"Because how else will we know what's in there, Mom?"—and how this compulsive reordering made her feel—"Like all is right with the world, Mom." Together they took the time to understand this strength and then to figure out productive ways to channel it.

Today, the daughter is a senior registered nurse who runs the level-one trauma unit for the largest hospital in the state of Tennessee. Here her compulsive attention to detail isn't a weakness to be fixed. It's now a strength that saves lives.

You must try to do the same with your specific strengths. Don't let anyone tell you that your strengths are weaknesses. Instead learn how to name, own, and channel your strengths so that all the rest of us can benefit from them.

TO GET BACK ON TRACK,
REMEMBER THE BEST ADVICE

1 Performance is always the point

So don't expect your organization ever to know you like you do.

2 Your strengths aren't what you're good at, and your weaknesses aren't what you're bad at

So you'd better find out what your real strengths are.

3 When it comes to your job, the "What" always trumps the "Why" and the "Who"

So always ask: "What will I be paid to do?"

4 You'll never find the perfect job

So every week, for the rest of your life, write your Strong Week Plan.

5 You'll never turn your weaknesses into strengths

So fess up to your weaknesses, then neutralize them.

THE TRUTH ABOUT YOU
YOUR SECRET TO SUCCESS

© 2008 by Marcus Buckingham

Published in Nashville, Tennessee, by Thomas Nelson. Thomas Nelson is a registered trademark of Thomas Nelson, Inc.

Produced by Dot+Cross and Kevin Small.

Thomas Nelson, Inc., titles may be purchased in bulk for educational, business, fund-raising, or sales promotional use. For information, please e-mail SpecialMarkets@ThomasNelson.com.

Library of Congress Cataloging-in-Publication Data

Buckingham, Marcus.
  The Truth About You : Your Secret To Success / Marcus Buckingham.
      p. cm.
  ISBN 978-1-4002-0226-3
  1. Success in business. 2. Success. 3. Employee motivation. I.
Title.
  HF5386.B8824 2008
  650.1—dc22   2008014562

Printed in China

08 09 10 11 12 RRD 9 8 7 6 5 4 3 2 1